Paul Daley is an author, journalist, essayist and short story writer. His books have been shortlisted for the Prime Minister's History Prize and ACT Book of the Year. He has won two Walkley Awards, two Kennedy Awards and the National Press Club Award for Excellence in Press Gallery Journalism. His essays have appeared in *Meanjin* and *Griffith Review* and he writes 'Postcolonial', a column for *The Guardian* about Australian national identity, history and Indigenous culture.

Writers in the *On Series*

Paul Daley

On
Patriotism

hachette
AUSTRALIA

For Honest History

Every attempt has been made to locate the copyright holders for material quoted in this book. Any person or organisation that may have been overlooked or misattributed may contact the publisher.

hachette
AUSTRALIA

Published in Australia and New Zealand in 2020
by Hachette Australia
(an imprint of Hachette Australia Pty Limited)
Level 17, 207 Kent Street, Sydney NSW 2000
www.hachette.com.au

First published in 2018 by Melbourne University Publishing

10 9 8 7 6 5 4 3 2 1

A catalogue record for this book is available from the National Library of Australia

ISBN: 978 0 7336 4412 2 (paperback)

Original cover concept by Nada Backovic Design
Text design by Alice Graphics
Author photograph by Mike Bowers
Typeset by Typeskill
Printed and bound in Australia by McPherson's Printing Group

PATRIOTISM, n. Combustible rubbish ready to the torch of any one ambitious to illuminate his name.

In Dr. Johnson's famous dictionary patriotism is defined as the last resort of the scoundrel. With due respect to an enlightened but inferior lexicographer I beg to submit that it is the first.

Ambrose Bierce, *The Devil's Dictionary* (1911)

Each year in the anodyne Melbourne suburb where I grew up, the nuns would order us to stand at attention, a little battalion of Catholic boys and girls, while the names of our relatives who'd died in the Great War were announced over the crackling public address system. Anzac Day was special for another reason: it was the only occasion that I can recall the Australian flag being raised at my primary school assembly.

It all felt alien to me—as inexplicable as those little cartons of free 'government milk', curdled and warm by mid-morning, that we were forced to drink daily because they were supposedly good for us. But those in charge knew best. And, just as we endured the milk, so, too, we stood and listened to the names of the dead spoken with utmost solemnity, staying still as attendant privates to avoid a crack behind the knees from a sister's ruler.

I had no Anzac blood—just an uncle who'd served overseas in World War II. Previous generations of my family's men had not done any fighting, except perhaps with fists on the footy field or on the streets of the Collingwood slum. My father was exempted from World War II because he worked on the Victorian railways, an essential service. It's doubtful, based on my later discussions with him, if he'd have gone anyway. Neither his father nor my mother's had volunteered to serve in the 1st Australian Imperial Force; both were staunch Irish republicans opposed to conscription at a time Australia was yoked to the Empire, wracked with sectarianism and divided with bitterness over plebiscites on whether to give prime minister Billy Hughes the power to conscript.

After the local member of parliament had laid his Anzac Day wreath at my school, there'd be much excited discussion, bragging really, I suppose, among the kids about men in their families who'd died in battle, or who'd returned from war with bits missing or thereafter never been quite right. Their families had experienced something that was as foreign to me as the places—Gallipoli, Fromelles, Palestine—where their soldiers had died. This experience had bypassed my family. I felt jibbed. I wanted to be included—but not quite as badly as some of my classmates whose families, similarly, had no claim to it either.

And, so, with each 25 April, more of my fellow pupils nominated a grandfather or perhaps a great-uncle who, they claimed, had died in battle. I think it became something of a sport, a high-risk deception of the nuns, to submit the name of your grandfather (who'd in fact died from a heart attack in his seventies while tending the roses in Glen Iris) and have it announced over the PA together with the names of those who were actually killed on the shores of the Dardanelles.

I do recall contemplating drafting my granddads. But I resisted this significant temptation; the prospect that the lie—*Harry Daley; Bill Bourke … killed in action*—would get back to my parents, who'd be furious, was probably enough to dissuade me, I suspect. And there was a terrible fuss when the nuns, realising the Gallipoli fatality list was still steadily growing half a century after the ill-fated Australian landing, sought parental clarification. By the next Anzac Day the school community's sacrifice had diminished.

The story of who we are—of where we came from and of the trails blazed by our ancestors—is everything. Even in my primary school years beginning in 1969, as our older siblings and cousins were burning draft cards and marching in the streets against Australia's part in another imperial war, Vietnam, Anzac already seemed secure, though not nearly as ostentatiously so as today, in our slowly evolving national narrative.

In 1964, the year of my birth, Donald Horne sketched in his polemic *The Lucky Country* a lackadaisical Australia, neither boldly republican nor imperialist. He wrote that thanks, perhaps, to the rise and defeat of European fascism, nationalism 'is now so hesitant that it no longer achieves self definition. No one any longer tells Australians who they are, nor do they seem to care'.[1]

'The very lack of any definite nationalism, of statements on who Australians are and where they stand in history, cannot be wholeheartedly deplored in an age that has seen so much horror and cruelty unleashed in the name of nationalism', he wrote.[2]

Despite this careless (or dozy) Australian sense of self, this lack of concern with nationalism, Horne nonetheless identified Anzac—'the Festival of the Ordinary Man'—as an understated yet critical tenet of national identity. It was, he wrote, perhaps because 'the whole process of achieving nationhood [through a bloodless federation] was so easy that, it was not until men died, if quite irrelevantly, and in a minor and unsuccessful campaign, that Australians felt they had earned their way into the world'.[3]

National birth had, it seemed, not only skipped 60 000-plus years of Indigenous continental habitation, it had also failed to incorporate Federation in 1901, an event that almost twelve decades later still sits in the outer stalls of public consciousness as little more than a big COAG meeting with beards.

Anzac Day, Horne reckoned, was 'an expression of the commonness of man (even death is a leveller), of the necessity for sticking together in adversity ... It is not a patriotic day but ... a "tribal festival", the folk seeing itself as it is—unpretentious and comradely'.[4]

Twenty-six years after the book that (despite his four subsequent novels and many non-fiction works) defined his legacy as a writer and public intellectual, in a long recorded interview with Film Australia's *Australian Biography* project, Horne defined nationalism as meaning

that you're a patriotic chauvinist, which means that you believe that your country is superior to other countries. There's no harm in people thinking that we'll win the Admiral's Cup, we've got Ayers Rock [Uluru] and so forth. That doesn't do much harm but it ... can become nasty and xenophobic ...[5]

Anzac Day, in Horne's words, was 'not a patriotic day' back around the time of my birth and that of his book. But things have since changed a great deal.

All the original Anzacs have gone. Most of their children are in their seventies and eighties, their grandchildren in their fifties and sixties. After my generation passes, there will be no living Australian memory of the soldiers who fought in World War I—nobody left to remember the ageing Anzacs on the trams, ferries and buses, worse for wear but for the most part dignified after commemorating together at their modest sunrise services before carrying on to play two-up in parks and pubs across Australia on their one day of the year. Their lives will be rendered with ever less human complexity, to become more storied and honed by an already vast army of mythologists. They will be further rendered soldier white hats who either stoically endured or who gave national birth while dying in battle, all the while bequeathing us fellow countrymen and women with supposedly unique characteristics of courage, ingenuity and mateship—traits that European/Australian myth has overlooked in all its enemies from the Ottomans, Germans and Japanese to the tens of thousands of Indigenous warriors and civilians slaughtered right here in the name of white settlement.

Back when Horne wrote his book, there was no rolling TV coverage of, and elaborate commentary on, the Anzac parades in the capital cities, events that lured a few thousand people in the sixties and seventies. Perhaps two or three hundred would turn up for the dawn services at the Shrine of Remembrance in Melbourne and the Australian War Memorial in Canberra— where crowds of 35 000 and 50 000, respectively, fronted on Anzac Day 2018.

But then again, 25 April 2018 represented peak Anzac—three-quarter time in a 51-month, $600-million carnival of Australian World War I commemoration that ended on 11 November: Remembrance Day. What was, when Horne wrote his 1964 book, a day of folksy, thoughtful reflection has been transformed into a permanent commemorative sound-and-light show. Any capacity for quiet reflection on the 62 000 who died in World War I, or the 102 000 defence personnel who've perished in all of this country's overseas operations, has been drowned out amid the type of boisterous jingoism and exclusive you-flew-here-we-grew-here style of nationalism that has imbued Australia Day with ever greater potency since the 1988 bicentenary.

Australia's spending on commemoration during the four years of Anzac 100 (this country's official commemorative program) has dwarfed that of other participant nations in World War I, even though other countries experienced many more combatant and civilian deaths. Australia has spent the equivalent of almost $9000 for every soldier killed, compared with far lower spending by the United Kingdom ($110 million, or $109 on each of its 1.01 million dead), New Zealand ($31 million, or $1713 on each of its 18 100 soldiers killed) and Germany (2.8 million fatalities, $6 million total, $2 on each).[6]

In the decades after the Great War, the returned services organisations had greater affinity with the conservative side of parliament. Today, no political party monopolises commemoration. Consecutive Labor and Coalition governments and their leaders over the past three-and-a-half decades (with the exception of Paul Keating) have increasingly clung to and conflated the Anzac myth with national foundation and identity. Anzac 100 has flourished, the ridiculous commitments to its funding announced, bolstered or unchallenged under prime ministers Kevin Rudd, Julia Gillard, Rudd again, Tony Abbott and now Malcolm Turnbull.

In 2015, the historian Peter Cochrane wrote, 'Drape "Anzac" over an argument and, like a magic cloak, the argument is sacrosanct'.[7]

A long tradition of obscurant political bipartisanship has protected Anzac's mythology and funding. It still shrouds Anzac with immunity from scrutiny over all manner of things—from the questionable proposition that Gallipoli is the foundry of the nation and its character, to the acceptance by Anzac's shrine, the Australian War Memorial, of funding from weapons manufacturers to commemorate our dead in foreign conflicts, while stubbornly ignoring the frontier wars that claimed, by some estimations, more Indigenous lives on this very continent than those of Australian soldiers killed between 1914 and 1918.

Australia's embrace of Anzac mythology, meanwhile, often seems more heavily moored in belief than fact. A prime example can be found in the words attributed to Mustafa Kemal Atatürk, a commander of Ottoman forces at the Dardanelles and later the founder of modern Turkey. The words grace memorials at Anzac Cove, Gallipoli, and on Anzac Parade, Canberra—testimony in statuary and bronze to the supposedly special relationship between Turkey and Australia and their respective national foundation myths, which both countries claim were forged in the Dardanelles furnace.

The words attributed to Atatürk are, in the most popular translation from the Turkish:

> Those heroes that shed their blood and lost
> their lives … You are now lying in the soil of
> a friendly country. Therefore rest in peace.
> There is no difference between the Johnnies

and the Mehmets to us where they lie side by side here in this country of ours ... You, the mothers who sent their sons from faraway countries, wipe away your tears; your sons are now lying in our bosom and are in peace. After having lost their lives on this land they have become our sons as well.

Heart-rending and full of comfort to the families of the Australian dead as they are, there's no proof Atatürk ever uttered or wrote these words. Indeed, there is more convincing evidence he did not. But like those who'd deny the compelling science of climate change, the sturdiest proponents of Anzac mythology do not require proof. Belief, it seems, is sufficient.

However, Peter Cochrane, who described Anzac as being sacrosanct in argument, also pointed out: 'History will not stand for that. In history nothing is sacred. History is open inquiry; politics is slogans'.[8]

Indeed, Anzac is not and should not be sacred, even though in death its soldiers have been sanctified and its language imbued with ecclesiasticism (think 'the spirit' and the 'glorious dead', and don't forget the 'sacrifice' of the 'fallen') that has shifted it from the realm of history to that of a secular religion in which the war memorial is its cathedral. As Australia prepared for Anzac 100, Vietnam veteran Jim Robertson wrote a submission to federal politicians urging them to

> try to avoid the utterly demeaning term 'fallen' when speaking of war dead—they did not trip over a stick or a garden hose,

they were drowned, burned, shot, gassed and eviscerated to lie face down in mud or sand or at the bottom of the ocean. War is human-kind's most horrific activity and it must be portrayed as such for that is how veterans see it. It should not be made to appear otherwise by false sensitivity or photos of politicians trying to look dutifully serious.[9]

They didn't listen to Jim. The politicians have been all over Anzac 100, even using it to justify engagement in new conflicts and to announce military hardware deals.

Anzac commemoration has become its own battleground—a new front, if you like, in a conflict over ideology and historical truth that began in 2001 about how the fledgling National Museum of Australia depicted the

frontier wars between British redcoats, settlers, pioneers, police, militias and civilian
hunting parties for Aboriginal people on the
one hand and, on the other, the Indigenes
who'd resisted them. Except to say that the
cultural conservatives were wrong in their
claim that progressives had exaggerated
Indigenous fatalities on the frontier, I'm not
going to re-run the so-called 'history wars'
here. But it is clear that, as Anzac assumed an
ever more inflated place in Australian cultural
and historical consciousness throughout the
late twentieth century and into this one, it
became something of a stage for an ideologi-
cal rematch.

On 26 April 2013, *The Australian* editorial-
ised about how those organising the centenary
celebrations for World War I might respond

to progressives who challenged the inflation of Anzac in Australian culture:

> The best advice we can offer is that they ignore the tortured arguments of the intellectuals and listen to the people, the true custodians of this occasion. They must recognise that the current intellectual zeitgeist is at odds with the spirit of Anzac. It recognises neither the significance of a war that had to be fought nor the importance of patriotism. Honour, duty and mateship are foreign to their thinking. They may be experts on many things, but on the subject of Anzac, they have little useful to say.[10]

By this rationale, those who questioned Anzac as the defining sentiment of Australian nationalism during the centenary would be at best unpatriotic. By implication, challenging or undermining the national sentiment built around Anzac would seem to be treasonous.

As Anzac 100 approached, I was wary of the galloping militarisation of my country's history. I had already had extensive dealings with Australia's armed forces as a defence correspondent. But I'd also made myself broadly conversant with our military history. In an attempt to understand even more what it was about Anzac that had come to so capture my nation's sentiments, I'd visited the World War I graves of Australians from Madang, Beersheba, Gaza and Tripoli to Gallipoli, Damascus, Bullecourt, Fromelles and beyond. Of course, I was touched by the individual stories associated with those rows upon rows of neat blonde stone tablets upon

which next of kin had just sixty-five characters (less than a tweet) to commemorate their
dead soldiers:

> How much of love and light and joy is bur-
> ied with our darling boy
> I've no darling now, I'm weeping baby
> and you left me alone
> Another life lost heart's broken for what

Who but the heartless could be unmoved
by this? The stories compelled me. I wrote
dozens of articles and several books about
men who served—the good and the bad, and
the many who had a complexion of both. I
felt—and still believe—that their stories
have enormous value for all they can teach
us about the human condition and, equally,
about the evils of war.

But they did not inspire in me any greater love of my country.

I was born lucky, coincidentally with Horne's book that took luck into its title and described so unsentimentally my good fortune to arrive on this earth Australian. Seeing so much of the world—its famished and its war victims, its frightened, oppressed and stateless—has of course reinforced my sense of providence. I've always loved living in Australia for all of the reasons that most of us do: its climate, physical beauty and abundance; its political freedoms and economic stability—its 'lifestyle'. But there are things I disdain too: its inequality and its refusal to acknowledge, let alone make amends for, the violent dispossession of its First Peoples; its demonisation of refugees; its vandalisation of the land and sea that sustain its beauty. Yes, I love much about Australia, but my relationship with this place is complex. It is a qualified love whose heartstrings are tangled in history and stories and beliefs that run far deeper than 1915 and 1788. For all of my traipsing around the overseas battlefields where the Anzacs fought, and through the militarily precise cemeteries of clipped buffalo grass and rosemary where they are buried, the essence of my country—that which I most love about it—was, of course, always right here at home.

It took me a long time to realise that. Then again, non-Indigenous Australia has always looked away from this continent for identity, first back to England and then, after the slaughter of the Dardanelles, to Gallipoli.

And as the carnival of Anzac 100 draws to a close, it remains ever the extrovert, content to seek national definition from its part in a failed invasion and occupation of an obscure finger of the Ottomans a century ago, yet increasingly closed to foreigners in need, advancing into a new millennia with a stubborn refusal to look inwards and reckon with all the historic pain and beauty that this continent harbours.

The bicentenary in 1988 was an awakening for me. It came as a moment of realisation that when the British invaded this continent, not only did they start dispossessing the Indigenous tribes from their land, they also began a parallel process of colonising their culture and their history. I sat at home in

Melbourne that 26 January anticipating the birth of my first daughter, whose arrival (a day after Anzac Day) would be celebrated with a specially minted bicentenary birth certificate. I watched on TV as thousands of Indigenous Australians protested around Sydney Harbour while replica tall ships sailed in with white 'settlers', replete with authentic costumes, to re-enact the invasion. I'd never thought much about Australia Day before; as a kid it had always seemed to me mainly a day for foreigners celebrating new citizenship— what one of my older cousins referred to as 'wogs and picnics day'. But 1988 brought home to me just how unreconciled a version of history my country was choosing to serve up to itself in this exclusive party for non-Indigenous Australia, whose celebrant in chief was the then Labor prime minister Bob Hawke. A few months later Hawke would promise Indigenous Australians a treaty. It was a hollow gesture, amounting to nothing.

Thirty years later, Australia is no closer to achieving Commonwealth treaties with the continent's custodians. Malcolm Turnbull's government, listing ever more to the right, as it did, while prime ministerial authority eroded, all but trashed the last vestiges of workable relations with First Nations through its crude dismissal of the appeal from Uluru in May 2017 for a process of national historical truth telling and an Indigenous voice to parliament. 'It's not going to happen', the then deputy prime minister Barnaby Joyce declared, oafish and obstreperous like some sunstruck bunyip sage, barely a day after the

Uluru Statement from the Heart urged legislators to walk with Indigenous people on this potential new path of conciliation.[11] It was, I believe, a tragic government misreading at a time when, three decades after the re-enactment of the invasion and 230 years post the real thing, a broad community and political debate about changing the date of Australia Day had opened up. In another three decades, when the child of my bicentenary daughter is herself thirty, the national day, if we have one, will not be on 26 January. I am certain of that.

Such ostentatious Australia Day patriotism had seemed to taper off somewhat after 1988 amid the talk of Hawke's treaty, land rights legislation that followed the High Court's Mabo ruling, and a change of tone regarding the First Nations under Keating, who in 1992 became the only prime minister to acknowledge the true darkness at the heart of our unsettled continental sovereignty:

> We took the traditional lands and smashed the traditional way of life. We brought the diseases. The alcohol.
>
> We committed the murders. We took the children from their mothers. We practised discrimination and exclusion. It was our ignorance and our prejudice. And our failure to imagine these things being done to us.
>
> With some noble exceptions, we failed to make the most basic human response and enter into their hearts and minds.[12]

There was a predictable correction to the right under John Howard. Barely a year into his prime ministership, he set the tone for the history wars when, at a reconciliation convention, he dismissed violent colonial dispossession as a mere blemish on the clean white pages of Australian history:

> In facing the realities of the past … we must not join those who would portray Australia's history since 1788 as little more than a disgraceful record of imperialism, exploitation and racism … such an approach will be repudiated by the overwhelming majority of Australians who are proud of what this country has achieved although inevitably acknowledging the blemishes in its past history.[13]

Delegates booed, turned their backs and hissed.

Howard wasn't acting alone. P Hanson of Ipswich, an electoral accident who quickly figured out how to tap the politics (and nationalism) of welfare envy, was already beating the tom-toms about the supposed privilege enjoyed by Aboriginal people, despite their 200-plus years of oppression and denied rights, and on levels of Asian migration. Hanson, like Howard, would adapt to the xenophobia of the times and shift sights, nimble as a sniper, to another soft target: Middle Eastern (mostly Muslim) refugees—they're still in the crosshairs of Hanson, now re-minted as a senator, and those in government who learned at Howard's feet.

Howard—whose father and grandfather served concurrently on the Western Front in World War I—fostered the values of Anzac while, in his second term, deploying troops to East Timor. He became a khaki prime minister, never more confident than when talking national and international security, especially border control.

I had moved to London by the end of Howard's second term, when the *Tampa*, filled with many persecuted Middle Eastern people, sailed into Australian waters. Howard eventually deployed the best of the best Australian troops, the Special Air Service, to keep the 433 asylum seekers out of Australia (some of the troops later would confide they felt that they'd been deployed cynically, for obvious partisan political purpose).[14]

I watched in London, live, on early morning television, as that second airliner struck the World Trade Center. Howard was in

Washington, where he invoked Australia's part in the Anzus Alliance, meaning we would go to war alongside the Americans, if that's what it took, to nail the terrorists who'd done this. Patriotism, in the United States and in Australia, was on the front foot.

Consistent with Ambrose Bierce's description of patriotism as 'combustible rubbish', it was now tinderbox dry.

Howard's declaration in the election campaign of late 2001 that 'we will decide who comes to this country and the circumstances in which they come' was a bald rejection of the fundamental tenets of global refugee policy. Still, it propelled him to a third term of office and set the parameters for the toxic politics of Australian border protection that burbles like deadly molten lava at the centre of major party politics today, and results in the detention of asylum seekers in hellish conditions away from the Australian mainland. The major parties' virtue vacuum on asylum seeker policy is a potent source of shame to me as an Australian citizen, not least because it means my country has surrendered significant moral authority regarding the treatment of refugees elsewhere, including the United States—just as it has surrendered its moral authority on Indigenous welfare and rights globally.

Before Australia Day 2003, I'd only twice noticed Australians wearing our national ensign as a cape: the first time involved the would-be politician Hanson in 1997; the second was at the Sydney Olympics in 2000, when Cathy Freeman wrapped herself in the

Aboriginal and Australian flags after winning gold in the 400 metres. By 2003 I'd lived for two years in South West London, home to hordes of expatriate antipodeans. Besides their accents and the occasional Barry McKenzie-ish affectation on the District Line after closing time of a Friday night, I'd never noticed any overt displays of Australian patriotism or flag fetishism. But that 26 January, something seemed different. Dozens wore Australian flags as capes. More had little flags stencilled on their faces and hands. The chants of 'Aussie, Aussie, Aussie' echoed into the cold night. It was harmless fun, but its extraordinariness was confounding. Since 9/11, the atmosphere and politics in Australia and Britain—only marginally less so than in the United States—had been charged with militarism. Australia was in a war (on terror) for the first time since its troops had been pulled out of Vietnam in 1972, having invaded Afghanistan as part of a US-led coalition, and it would soon take a leading role in the invasion of Iraq. Every day, the British media were saturated with stories about which countries would be involved in the Iraq incursion, and whose troops (Australian special forces were mentioned regularly) had been in the heaviest fighting in Afghanistan.

Back home, the boats kept arriving, their occupants mostly from the Middle East, where Australian troops were fighting. They were refugees demonised by the major parties, tainted with suspicion due to the more extreme anti-Muslim rhetoric of the war on terror, and banished to remote islands from where they'd never ever reach Australia.

In 2005 Khaki Howard visited Gallipoli for the ninetieth anniversary of that invasion:

> History helps us to remember but the spirit of Anzac is greater than a debt to past deeds. It lives on in the valour and the sacrifice of young men and women that ennoble Australia in our time, in scrub in the Solomons, in the villages of Timor, in the deserts of Iraq and the coast of Nias. It lives on through a nation's easy familiarity, through Australians looking out for each other, through courage and compassion in the face of adversity.[15]

In the stifling early days of the Sydney summer that same year, it was as if the circuitry of sentiment around Anzac, the flag, terrorism, immigration, border control and Australian nationalism had suddenly melted down and exploded into twenty-four hours of violence between Middle Eastern and other young men in the Sutherland Shire. Here, the flag was appropriated as a 'Cronulla cape' by those casting themselves as defenders of the beach, that mythic social plane that supposedly symbolises our egalitarianism— especially in Sydney, the most visually hedonistic of Australian cities, with its character motifs of lifesavers, sand, surf and a vivid blue sky.

Rarely, except in wartime, has the Australian flag been used to evoke such territorial aggression, as illegitimate as it was. For at Cronulla the Australian flag became a symbol of violent claim and exclusion, a hideous distillation of Anglo-Australian racism that exposed the ugliest expressions of our patriotism. A seventeen-year-old boy of Lebanese extraction climbed the flagpole outside Brighton-Le-Sands RSL Club, stole the Australian flag and burned it. This earned him the ire of a lynch mob (from which he was saved), a conviction and incarceration for malicious damage, and excoriation in the more hateful extremities of tabloid and shock-jock commentary. He apologised publicly, even demonstrating his repentance and rehabilitation by walking the Kokoda Track in Papua New Guinea (another place, like Gallipoli, revered for its apparent contribution to national character) at the behest of the returned services organisation. The intent was to coach the boy on the link between Australian military 'sacrifice' and the blue ensign (especially when flown outside an RSL). Nonetheless, *The Daily Telegraph* gave him a gratuitous touch-up, a reminder he'd 'committed the ultimate insult' to Australians, which had made him 'public enemy No 1'.[16]

That ought to teach him!

The crowd at Cronulla evoked Anzac and Gallipoli on 11 December 2005. Like this: 'You're standing on the soil that has been fought for by Australian Anzac diggers'. And this: 'This is what our grandfathers fought for, to protect this, so we can enjoy it, and we don't need these Lebanese or wogs to take it away from us'.[17]

It's instructive that some of the more probing, immediate mainstream media analysis of the perverted patriotism displayed at Cronulla, and its conflation with race hate and Anzac, seemed to come from overseas. Yes, acres of newsprint and hours of television were devoted to the social contributors to the riots—the harassment of women on the beach and the subsequent clashes between Lebanese-Australian men and lifesavers, who were also likened to the combatants at Gallipoli; the flames fanned by media reactionaries and xenophobes. But there was little domestic media focus on the poisonous melding of Anzac myth, the flag and anti–Middle Eastern sentiment.

New South Wales RSL president Don Rowe did tell the BBC World Service:

We were absolutely disgusted. That is the last thing that Anzac is interpreted as being. The Anzac spirit is mateship, looking after one another … you certainly don't go around waving flags and call yourself an Anzac and go around belting people up. That's totally the opposite to what Anzac is.[18]

Rowe had wanted the young flag burner to carry the blue ensign during a subsequent Anzac Day parade; many thought that there could be no better demonstration of post-riot reconciliation. But Rowe had to scrap that plan after receiving serious threats.

The ferocious, ugly display at Cronulla, with its misappropriation of Anzac and the flag, was more redolent of Horne's 1964 reference to other nations where 'patriotic chauvinism' could become 'nasty and xenophobic'. This bore no resemblance to the 'hesitant nationalism' he'd identified in Australia.

There were inquiries, of course. But Australia went back to the beach without parsing adequately the political and cultural contributors to the riot, its dangerous commandeering of national symbols in the name of exclusionary violence—and most of all, the lessons that might be carried forward. The failure to comprehend or the refusal to embrace what happened is illustrated starkly thirteen years later by refugee policy where the national realpolitik discourse has cornered itself in a dark space, one where excessive compassion for asylum seekers is a liability to be weighed against public fears over border control and the terrorism of Islamic extremism. The history wars that began at the National Museum have broadened and shifted into other cultural and political landscapes, but have never, in my view, petered out. They encompass divisions between public intellectuals, historians, journalists, writers and artists over a range of issues, all of which concertina, contribute to national character and historical consciousness, and cleave public sentiment. They still swirl around the denial of Indigenous rights, truth telling about frontier violence, memorialisation of the revered British responsible for its worst excesses, and the continued celebration of 26 January—just as they now incorporate the division over the rights and treatment of refugees, and any challenge to the dominant national creation myth and commemorative focus of Anzac.

Romantic love, its capacity to make us trust and surrender, defies our intelligent powers of rationality and logic. It can become as debilitating and deleterious as an illness when its astigmatism blinds us to necessary or hurtful truths.

But love can also provoke our self-awareness and inspire us to check our vulnerabilities against truth. No love is perfect, but a love based on the truth is the strongest. Anyone who says otherwise is lying.

So it is with patriotism—the love of one's country.

At 4 a.m. one day a few years ago, I set sail onboard an old pearling boat into a seemingly endless expanse of the black Arafura Sea, just as the first crimson bolts of dawn began to crack the leaden sky. It was perfectly still and quiet but for the monotonous, calming

hum of the diesel engine and the gulls caw-
ing above. As the boat progressed and dawn
transformed the sky into a luminous tan-
gerine canvas, as silver fish streaked and
skipped across the water's skin, and while
terns hovered on the currents at our tail, I felt
like I was traversing an invisible border into
another universe. In so many ways, most of
us onboard were. I couldn't help wondering
whose hands—those of the captain or some
higher being?—held our fate.

We were sailing about sixty sometimes
treacherous nautical miles from Gove in
north-east Arnhem Land to the island of
Raragala, uninhabited these days but once
the childhood home of the Yolngu warrior,
law man and spiritual keeper of the *yidaki*
(didjeridu), Djalu Gurruwiwi. Djalu, then

aged in his eighties, was with us. So, too, was his wife Dhopiya, his even more frail elder and since departed sister Dhanggal, and her two dogs, his five children, three nieces and grandson. It did not pay to countenance the multitude of things that might go wrong.

As I leaned on the railing and looked out while we passed the promontory of one of the many small islands in the Wessel group, Dhanggal explained to me just how dangerous this journey could be. She had prayed to the spirit of the dog 'over there', incarnate in the giant protruding red boulder we could see on the point. The dog safeguarded the straits from strangers to the Yolngu clans. In a few hours, she said, we would sail through a narrow channel named 'the hole in the wall', whose waters could suddenly boil up into a series of waves and whirlpools that had sucked hundreds of wayfarers into their dark depths over tens of thousands of years. A serpent guarded it. The dog had created that headland, the serpent the channel—both had always lived there. Dhanggal and Djalu had prayed to them both to deliver safe passage to the Yolngu and their *balanda* visitors on the boat. Once we got to Raragala, we could worry about the snakes, the restless spirits of invaders who'd died there, and the mutant gorilla (in which she did not believe but many other Yolngu do) supposedly inhabiting a cave at the northern end of the island.

I became anxious and tense, alive to a new consciousness about the animated landscape. I'd read widely and spoken to many Aboriginal and Torres Strait Islander people in an attempt to understand Indigenous spirituality. But this voyage would open my eyes to just how practically, how prosaically, Indigenous spiritual belief intersects with the everyday.

In that sense, my passage through the hole in the wall would become the key to a far greater understanding of Indigenous spirituality and culture. It would challenge me to think about how I related to my country—yes, in a national (or Commonwealth) sense, but more importantly, emotionally, spiritually, cosmologically and biologically.

After two days of music and storytelling on the island, of introspection and exploration, of avoiding the snakes (and the gorilla), we headed for the mainland. I sat at the bow that calm afternoon as we re-entered the hole in the wall for the return journey. Suddenly, the wind began to yowl and cry. The water churned as the channel rose and fell, waves crashing onto the deck from a dozen directions. I felt safe in the hands of the captain, experienced in those waters, and confident in the sturdiness of her boat. And I knew the Yolngu had once again sought and received permission from the creationist animals and spirits to pass.

But Dhanggal summonsed me to the aft of the boat and into the cabin, where she, Dhopiya, Djalu, the nieces and the other *balanda* stood in a circle. They made room for me and we linked hands as the boat rocked madly about and the engine roared and screamed. I followed the others and bowed my head as Djalu prayed in Yolngu: 'God the almighty who controls power … give us all and our visitors too a safe crossing over our waters and back to our land. Praised be to God and hallelujah'.

I later asked Dhanggal where God and Christianity fitted into a belief system that included creationist animals. She said I 'shouldn't forget Islam, also' because the Muslim trepang fishermen from Macassar had introduced their religion to the Yolngu perhaps hundreds of years before the Europeans—the Dutch, Portuguese, and later the British—had laid eyes on the continent's northern coastline. She said, 'God was there in the beginning and we always believed in the spirit. God the creator was always there and he is there in the songlines and in the stories of the land. And he has been reintroduced to us again through the missions. It's not complicated for us'.

Here was a belief system, one so layered, so storied, so beautiful, at once so complex and simple, that incorporated the story of the creation of a universe, which is to say all of the land and sea and sky in Yolngu experience. Faith for the Yolngu, and so many of the continent's other Indigenous peoples, not only incorporates but embraces what most others might regard as an untidy, illogical narrative of competing beliefs and stories. For the Yolngu, they are all elements of a whole that draws on 60 000-plus years of continental civilisation.

In the Australian quest to determine who and what we are, did our political and cultural leaders ever draw on this inner wellspring of

complexity and beauty for a character or—
better still—a story of formative nationalism
to project outward to the world? No. Instead,
they've confected a national foundation myth
around two experiences drawn from overseas: 1788 and Anzac.

The moment for a greater national
introspection—a search for and of the soul, if
you like—is long, long overdue. It is time to
also invest our patriotism with the profound
cosmological and cultural depths of this
Australia, a place we all call our 'country'—
our understanding of which varies dramati-
cally. In part, that depends on whether we are
Indigenous or not. Indigenous people who
are in touch with traditional culture, whether
they live in the cities, rural areas or remotely,
are conversant with the multilayered textural

meanings of *country* that both underlay and supersede its application to an Australian nation-state. But the profound historical, cultural and spiritual meaning is not closed to non-Indigenous people who make the effort to listen, travel and discover.

My friend John Carty grew up and went to school in the same innocuous, politically conservative eastern suburbs Bible belt of Melbourne as me. He is now the head of anthropology at the South Australian Museum in Adelaide, keeper of the biggest collection of Australian Indigenous cultural material in the world. He spent years in the central Australian deserts and in Arnhem Land, listening, asking and learning about Aboriginal art and culture. This enabled him to come up with a definition of *country*, in the English language, that encapsulates the explanations various Indigenous peoples have offered him.

Carty once gave a speech where he said:

I'm talking about *country* as a concept that gets thrown around every day in art and museum circles but is rarely used or interrogated with the seriousness that it deserves. I'm not talking about country in political terms, of nation-state, nor aesthetic country in terms of a neutral landscape … [*Country*] in the translation from various Aboriginal words such as *Ngurra* into English has a depth of meaning far exceeding its common usage. It is a political and aesthetic phenomenon but it is also so much more. *Country* is a kind of memory—it is memory laid down by the lives of one's family, by the events of one's childhood, by the journeys of one's ancestors, and by the tensions and conflicts of a changing world. Historical, mythological, familial and personal narratives are all layered, sedimented, in places where they happened. They are not separated out into different moments in time or categories of reality.

I didn't read Horne's *The Lucky Country* until it and I turned fifty. That was when, after the death of the legendary *Sydney Morning Herald* writer and editor Peter Bowers, his son Mike bequeathed me a mint-condition second edition that had belonged to his father, one of Australia's finest journalists— a contemporary of Horne—who I'd long admired for his courage and iconoclasticism.

The modest, folksy, everyman's Anzac Day that Horne depicts is unrecognisable against the current politicians' festival of World War I centenary commemoration. It's doubtful if the writer himself would have known it. Certainly, it would've been anathema to the veterans who, true to the nature of Anzac Day since it was first observed in 1916, saw it as a time for personal reflection—an emotion-letting, boozy catharsis, yes, but more often undertaken with no higher purpose than the opportunity it afforded to be among those who shared the same unspoken understanding of how war's catastrophic experience irrevocably reshapes its survivors and freights them with guilt.

Bill Gammage's 1974 book *The Broken Years* is based on the writings of a thousand men who fought in World War I. It lays bare the damage done to the Australian fighting men, exposing how the pro-British sentiment and Australian patriotism extant in the soldiers in 1914 had dissolved into despair and lament by war's end. The cauldron of Gallipoli, the blame of its disasters sheeted home to English command (when, in fact, so many of the disasters, such as the Battle of the Nek, were partly attributable to Australian command), certainly fomented an anti-British sentiment on the battlefield and on the home front. But there is little evidence in Gammage's book—or in the diaries and letters of hundreds of other soldiers that I've read—that the men's disenchantment with British command was somehow the genesis of some more independent-minded spirit of pervasive Australian patriotism. If anything, a strong brand of anti-British—indeed, even republican—nationalism gathered around the anti-war rather than the pro-war movements during the (defeated) conscription plebiscites of 1916 and 1917.

Private Charles Hardy of the 1st Australian Imperial Force's 19th Battalion is one of the tens of thousands of men who kept extensive diaries during the war—his are in the Mitchell Library in Sydney. In late 1915, as the Empire's troops prepared to retreat from Gallipoli, Hardy wrote in his leather-bound, flock-patterned address book:

Your King Your Country
Needs You
This is how they treat you
Oi Oi not a Game

Not a game it is
Oi Oi

As a teenager, I began to get some sense of all this from a book that my anti-war father gave me—the novel *My Brother Jack* by George Johnston, whose publication was also coincidental to my birth year. I was doing secondary school history, which was all presented as very straightforward: Captain Cook 'discovered' Australia; 1788 brought white 'settlement' and 'European civilisation' to the continent, after which 'the aborigine' just disappeared; Federation was an unremarkable inevitability for the British colonies; and the nation was born at Gallipoli and carried forward that fighting spirit to defeat the 'Japs' who'd been intent on invading and colonising Australia.

World War I was alluded to as the national tragedy it was for the loss of 62 000 Australian men and the wounding of 200 000 more. We drilled quite deeply into its geopolitical and economic impact and history (although it never did make sense to me how this four-year, three-month cataclysm could, by war's end, be seen to have simultaneously ushered the seventeen-year-old federation and a generation of its men to such a brink while also defining its nationhood). But my schoolboy lessons avoided the Great War's social impact; we were not encouraged to explore the legacy bequeathed to the veterans, the permanently debilitated and the families of the dead.

Indeed, the men came home after both world wars to just bloody well get on with it while Australia continued the real work of nation-building. That was that.

Johnston, who spent a life dwelling on notions of masculine 'courage', inspired my curiosity by picking at that scab in this book my dad gave me with the commendation that 'here is a writer who conveyed what war really did to this country and its people'. He introduced me to an Australia that was scarred—and remains so—by its experiences in the world wars. Johnston created the hallway at Avalon, the family home of his protagonist David Meredith (also in a 'dreary' suburb near my own), replete with prosthetic legs and walking sticks for the disabled veterans who were always about (Meredith's mother was a nurse, his father a Gallipoli vet). He wrote about how physically complete men 'were petty rare beings—complete that is, in that they had their sight or hearing or all their limbs. Well, we knew they existed, but they seldom came our way'.[19] Rather, there were blokes like Meredith's brother-in-law, Bert, an amputee confined to a convalescent hospital for a recovery that never advanced.

Inspired partly by this, I'd later seek out in my non-fiction and journalism the stories that were counterfactual to the Anzac myth— of the men and women whose lives were ruined in a fledgling federation that stoically bolted its front doors to hide the shameful domestic violence, the terrified kids, the morphine addiction and the venereal disease and untouched dinners of Anzac.

I hated war. But I also found it—and especially the (mostly) men who fought it—compelling. So as a journalist, I sought out occasional opportunities to travel to theatres of conflict in Europe, the Pacific and South-East Asia. I enjoyed the insights afforded me through mixing with and interviewing operational Australian troops.

One day in 1999, I sat with Australian troops on the verandah of a burned-out building in the high forested country behind Dili, the capital of East Timor, recently razed and emptied of its population by the Indonesian military and its militias. When I asked the soldiers what was important, most nominated loyalty to mates in the field above all else. There was much discussion of different illnesses and minor injuries, the monotony of ration packs, of slow mail and of missing home and family. They'd had frightening skirmishes with militias. Most seemed free of false bravado; some wore heavily their emotion over the recent discovery of the corpses of villagers—including a child—who'd been murdered. They were overwhelmed with curiosity about whether people back home recognised the importance of what they were doing, and they were gratified at my answer that, yes, perhaps no other Australian deployment since Federation had received so much public support. They were mindful of the geopolitical and human importance of their endeavours. They would not have chosen to be anywhere else.

There was also talk of history. Some felt Anzac freighted them with too much expectation to be ideal soldiers—strong, resourceful and stoic—like the originals. I hadn't expected this. Similarly telling was the palpable contempt for the politicians who'd sent them; some said that while they were absent from family and endangering them-selves, others might be wringing electoral and public credit from their actions.

It was hard to argue. I got an even greater sense of this in the years to come when I wrote extensively about the scourge of post-traumatic stress disorder and other combat-related afflictions in returned services personnel, and the legal and bureaucratic battles they fought for compensation and recognition.

The Howard government's East Timor deployment had come reluctantly (although it was always presented as otherwise) amid immense pressure from the United States, to which Howard would later pledge to be a 'deputy sheriff'. But the critical part played by the Australian INTERFET force in liberating East Timor from Indonesia and creating a new democratic country proved electorally popular in Australia. It represented Howard's arrival as a PM with a strong military affiliation, a reputation enhanced during Australia's war-on-terror military deployments and manifest in his political manoeuvring around border control and asylum seekers.

It was also the birth of a new Australian military hero in Peter Cosgrove, commander of the international forces in East Timor. Since 2014, Cosgrove has been Australia's nominal head of state—one of many career soldiers, and the second in six years, to be appointed governor-general.

When I worked at *The Bulletin* magazine in its dying final four years, I did so with a strong sense of its literary past. It felt as if those giants of editors such as Horne—who removed the tagline 'Australia for the White Man' from the magazine's cover only in the early 1960s—and JF Archibald, and writers like Harry 'The Breaker' Morant, Banjo Paterson and Henry Lawson, had created a cultural institution of incomparable literary value about which their ghosts still (meta-phorically) rattled. Such was the weight of history about the place. Political and social iconoclasm, even during those final years, was a mainstay, and whenever I went rural to research an article, I couldn't help but be touched by the sentiment and nostalgia people held for these writers—especially Lawson—who'd died so long ago.

Both Paterson—who'd fought in the Transvaal and worked in the light horse remounts during the Great War—and Lawson wrote of an Australia that was (rightly or apocryphally) defining patriotism according to man's connection to the country—its bush and nation-status—by stumping, droving, cropping, building, and battling the snakes and fires. Their fellows were a new, egalitarian, tough, resilient breed of men, British but distinctly *Australian*, defined by the bush and the elements and ready at any time to stand independently of the Empire. I sensed them about the place, even if their characters never quite rang

true to me. But women (unlike in the stories of
female *Bulletin* alumnae Barbara Baynton and
Katharine Susannah Prichard) rarely featured
in their work ('The Drover's Wife' is excep-
tional), despite the hardships they endured in
colonial and post-Federation rural and urban
Australia. And Aboriginal people, despite all of
the violence that had happened on the frontier
and the complex black–white relationships that
developed, featured largely as literary staffage,
incidental and accessories to white men, often
half-touched, hopeless and God-fearing fringe
dwellers devoid of culture.

Lawson was self-conscious about this
omission. One of the stories that made his
name, 'The Bush Undertaker' of 1892,
depicts an old shepherd respectfully re-
burying a white mate and digging up the

remains of a blackfella. It's an allusion to the widespread, shameful industry that emerged on the frontier around the theft and sale of Indigenous remains to anatomy schools and collecting institutions throughout the world. A goanna, lumbering with allegory, enters the story; white conscience—or lack of—perhaps.

Bunurong writer Bruce Pascoe observed:

Henry Lawson, who ignored Aboriginal people, wrote the great poem 'Faces in the Street', and every time I'm in a city, part of my journey is in step with the rhythm of that poem, 'drifting past, drifting past, to the beat of weary feet'. But Lawson was thinking of the noble white poor, they were his heroes, whereas he lived in a world where the broken armies of black resistance were scattered in the streets about him; yet one of the only times he mentioned them was to condemn them as cheats and scoundrels in *The Drover's Wife*.[20]

The owner of *The Bulletin*, Kerry Packer, not much inclined to sentiment, however sentimental he was about the magazine, more perhaps for its political influence than its cultural import, shuffled off into his assured nothingness ('let me tell you, there's fucking nothing there'), leaving it all in the hands of son James, the melancholy prince with a preference for gambling palaces over press baronry. James sold it to a private equity company that saw in *The Bulletin* nothing of value, cultural or financial. When the magazine closed, so, too, for me did a door on two decades of full-time journalism. I fell on the cheque and hot-footed it to the Middle East and Europe and into the Australian archives. But this time, on the old battlefields and in the cemeteries of Israeli-occupied Palestine (including Gaza), Israel itself, Jordan, Lebanon and Syria, I wasn't chasing news but rather stories from history about the Australians who'd been there in World War I. I thought if I could see where they'd fought and died, if I examined the raw materials of their stories in the archives in London and Canberra, I'd get closer to a more holistic Anzac from which Australia had patriotically cherrypicked.

During multiple trips to the Middle East, I wandered for weeks retracing the battles of the Australian Light Horse, precursors—for all their agility, bushcraft and warrior ability—to today's SAS. I developed a knack when walking amid the ubiquitous eucalypts (introduced to fight erosion around the wadies, a constant sensory reminder of home) and dust of old battle sites, like that on the semi-urban outskirts of the big, inhospitable Israeli Negev desert city Be'er Sheva, host to the devil-may-care 1917 charge of Beersheba, of finding old shrapnel and pieces of saddlery, bullet casings and bone.

Meanwhile, in the archives, I found the voices of Anzacs who'd been at Gallipoli and in Palestine, men who'd gone home to enjoy lives as respected citizens, 'good', 'solid' men in their communities—the same men who, in Palestine, had helped massacre all the men and many boys over sixteen in an Arab village and in a nearby camp of nomadic Bedouin. Like all humans they were complex, imperfect. They were Anzacs.

The diaries and letters of the men who took part in the three-year push against the Turks from the Suez Canal to their defeat and surrender at Damascus—the last stage of which, under command of the esteemed Australian cavalryman Harry Chauvel, was known as 'the great ride'—often stood out for their invective about the town Arabs and Bedouin. They and their more senior officers, especially those who'd come from the land, often portrayed them as inferior beings and compared them with the Aboriginal people they'd encountered back home. Henry Gullett reflected such sentiments in his official history of the Great War in the Middle East, writing that the Bedouin were scarcely 'higher in civilisation than the Australian blacks ...'.[21]

Of course, this attitude towards the Bedouin and the town Arabs instructed the Australians involved in the massacre at war's end in Surafend—a crumbling pile of rubble in Israel that was under development by the time I found it —which, when it was detailed in my book *Beersheba*, prompted a denial that it had ever happened from the RSL. Unfortunately for the organisation, Gullett in his history (along with Banjo Paterson in his dispatches and Patsy Adam-Smith in her hagiographic *The Anzacs*) had dealt with the massacre, albeit cursorily and as an aberration; more torching and killing of a similar nature at the hands of the Anzacs would follow in Egypt. When I wrote my book, I didn't think to invert my inquiries, to focus on the Australia from which the light horsemen had come and the treatment of those, back home, who they'd viewed—by Gullett's own estimation—as lower in civilisation.

Frontier conflict—massacres and indiscriminate shootings of Aboriginal men and women, and other widespread violence against them—was still a prominent feature of black–white relationships in Australia during World War I. The last mass killing of Aboriginal people is said to have happened at Coniston in the Northern Territory in 1928 (this does not account for deaths in custody). Its perpetrator was constable George Murray, a light horseman who fought at Gallipoli and later on the

European Western Front. After his inevitable acquittal (no white men were convicted of killing Indigenous people in frontier conflict in the twentieth century), Murray was lionised as a courageous patriot. In a 1933 newspaper feature, the novelist and journalist Ernestine Hill described Murray as the

> leader of the last of the great punitive police raids that alone have made for the safety of the white man in a black man's country … Occasional murders by the blacks in 60 years of history have inevitably been followed by drives of vengeance on the part of police and settlers … skulls and skeletons in their hundreds have commemorated many a wholesale massacre.[22]

Hill's idea of commemoration, whereby the very act of reprisal murder—and not the dead themselves—is symbolically memorialised with scattered bones, is as chilling as it is telling. Commemoration is the conscious act of remembering. It involves deliberate choices, such as what to forget. The Australian nation continues to be drawn, moth-like, unquestioning, to the light of Anzac and 1788 (and only ever their good bits) when it comes to the patriotic expression of its nationalism.

But what of those Indigenous people who sought to defend *black man's country*, as Hill concedes it was, from the police and settlers? Were not they this continent's first true patriots?

The land underfoot is furrowed and wind-blasted, sunbaked and hardened, so that it resembles a vast expanse of thousands of horizontal concrete rivulets. Grass stubble, so dry it crunches under my leather soles like cornflakes spilled on the kitchen floor, renders what had been a verdant stock paddock into an expanse of corrugated beige leading to a copse of eucalypts. There's no activity here now, save for the whirly-whirls of dust—and the spirits, of course, always the spirits of the dead.

Above is the navy blue of our flag, punctuated here and there with scudding white clouds that promise little but deliver less. It hasn't rained out here for months. It's not likely to. This country has always been dry. You and your animals can coexist with it, providing you embrace the long-term cycles of drought and plenty, but it's not for single-generation short-termers. You've got to honestly understand and worship this land like a lifelong lover, for all of its cruelty and beauty and bounty, to survive on it.

There is a tree. It is ancient and silver in death, its multiple branches twisting and twirling upwards like the arms of a Hindu deity. It stood here as witness when the burials took place and that's why the spirits of the dead still swirl around it. You might hear them if you stand still, their voices in the wind as they cry out to warn us strangers away.

Something clicks under the toe of my boot. I take a step back and look down at my footprint in the dust. It's a small piece of pointed stone, its edges chipped and crafted into blades. I walk a few steps and shuffle my foot about the dust and uncover another cutting tool.

At the beckoning of Dinawan Dyirribang, I wander over to a small oasis of younger eucalypts that are fenced off from the sheep that graze here when there's feed. He pulls an offshoot from one of the trees and brushes us three whitefellas with it, one by one, front and back, while chanting in his language. 'The old fella's over there near that tree. I see him. This is his land. He's suspicious, so I'm telling him it's all good', says Dinawan, a Wiradjuri elder who lives on the outskirts of Bathurst in central-west New South Wales, where he is also known as Uncle Bill Allen.

We follow him to a plot, its borders marked with the type of low fencing ubiquitous around kids' playgrounds, comprising smooth, green-stained wooden logs. Inside the plot are two gentle mounds, a pastiche of struggling cut grass and earth. At the front stands a metal plaque on a rustic plinth of roughly moulded concrete. Atop the plinth is a Wiradjuri axehead—one of many artefacts found here at Brucedale, a pastoral property for six generations of the Suttors since 1822, and now the oldest continuous family business in Australia. The plaque is dedicated to Windradyne, a Wiradjuri warrior who led guerrilla parties against the redcoats and settlers during the Bathurst War.

Windradyne is a Wiradjuri hero. Stories of his resistance to the British soldiers that the NSW governor, Thomas Brisbane, sent to protect the ever-expanding settlement of Bathurst, and the pastoralists who made claims there, are told as if they happened yesterday rather than when martial law was declared in 1824. Tensions between the Wiradjuri and the soldiers, settlers and shepherds had been simmering for the decade since another governor, Lachlan Macquarie (despite white history having afforded him a benign reputation, a butcher of Aboriginal people around Sydney), had raised the British flag at Bathurst in 1815. The settlers took traditional hunting grounds to graze stock. The Wiradjuri, deprived of their livelihood from the grasslands and the rivers, stole the stock. The redcoats and settlers killed the thieves with gunshot and widespread poisoning, and the warriors killed the soldiers, settlers and shepherds—a cycle of violent reprisals that defined frontier war across the continent until the twentieth century.

In 1824 came the infamous 'potato patch incident', when Windradyne's wife and several others were shot dead for taking potatoes from a plot on the Macquarie River from which they'd been offered the tubers the day before. This is how the Bathurst War began. Windradyne and his warriors wanted revenge. They turned up at Brucedale wearing war paint and brandishing their spears. The master, George Suttor, was away. It was his son, William, who greeted the men. The younger Suttor had learned the Wiradjuri language and, like his father, acknowledged that the local Aboriginal people had sovereignty over the land—including theirs. Windradyne and his family, and other local tribes, had often camped at Brucedale, where they coexisted in peace and mutual respect with the Suttors—so much so that during the Bathurst War, the Aboriginal people considered the property neutral territory.

One of William Suttor's sons, William Henry, would later write:

> He spoke to them in their own language in such a manner as not to let them suppose he anticipated any evil … They stood there, sullen, silent, motionless. My father's cheerful courage and friendly tone disarmed animosity. They consulted in an undertone, and departed as suddenly and as noiselessly as they came. The next thing known of them is they killed (was it not retribution) all the men at a settler's place some miles distant, the very place, where it was rumoured, the poison bread had been laid for them.[23]

The authorities put a price on Windradyne and he went into hiding, but the massacring and poisoning of his people continued apace under martial law. In late 1824 Windradyne emerged from the bush to walk over the Blue Mountains to Parramatta, together with a hundred or so of his warriors, where Brisbane pardoned him. It was Windradyne's way of saving his remaining people. In 1829 he was wounded in the leg during a conflict with a related tribe (to do, his descendants maintain, with internecine relations between the red-coats and some rival blacks). After leaving the Bathurst Hospital, he returned to Brucedale, where he died of gangrene.

Almost two centuries later, we are sitting on the verandah of Brucedale, looking down across the pastures to a row of tall, unkempt pear trees—perhaps the oldest of their type in Australia. David Suttor, a direct descendant of the original settler, George, examines while passing from hand to hand a stone artefact he recently found as he mustered his sheep. He hands it to Dinawan, who is a direct descendant of Windradyne.

'This one looks pretty old, I'd say, maybe a couple of hundred years', says Dinawan. 'What are you going to do with it?'

'You can have it, or I can hang onto it here for safekeeping', David replies.

'Yeah, you keep it', says Dinawan, handing the axehead back to his friend.

These men have been mates for years, continuing a tradition of amity that began between their families in a time of black–white war that turned the country around here into a battlefield—a stage for skirmishes between the Wiradjuri and the settlers and soldiers, reprisal attacks by Aboriginal guerrilla groups, and payback massacres and poisonings (William Henry Suttor wrote that the latter were part of a British plan for 'extermination' of the blacks). Together, they have worked to ensure that the site's Indigenous heritage is officially protected. The grave is listed on the state's heritage register, while the National Parks and Wildlife Service has fenced off the site to protect it from livestock, and erected storyboards about Windradyne.

David says, 'We had that [grave] site there and we wanted formal recognition of it and we had to make sure it is preserved. So it was never a fear thing that they're going to take our land. We've always had a relationship with the Wiradjuri and we will continue it and hopefully strengthen it by saying, "Let's make this a formal agreement that can never be desecrated by anyone in the future"'.

Dinawan says, 'We've kept that relationship open and we don't interfere with what David does, but we are on very good terms with each other, we can talk about things … like we joke about how one day we will get this land back …'.

The men laugh. But the dry is taking its toll on the Suttor business and the country that sustains it.

Later, as I'm leaving Brucedale, David Suttor says, 'You've got to take a long-term view of it all, especially when you're in a situation like this. I feel a duty to farm it responsibly and to leave the land in better shape when I hand it on than it was in when I started farming. I love the country here, it's why you stay. But I've only ever seen myself and the others before me as custodians, caretakers, of this place'.

And so he continues to farm the land just as, almost 200 years after George Suttor arrived, the Wiradjuri continue to come and go. The property is not subject to a native title claim, but it doesn't need to be for the Indigenous peoples' connection to the land to be acknowledged by those farming it. The story of the Wiradjuri and Brucedale is nothing if not one about a shared, albeit complex, at times tense, though amicable post-invasion black–white history—about an abiding love of country that transcends the racial divide. David Suttor, descended from generations of white farmers whose compassion compelled them to understand the land's custodians, has a living appreciation of how Brucedale—with its millennia of civilisation history, its continuing Wiradjuri spiritual significance, its storied boulders and trees—is, as Carty described *country*, a repository of others' memories and experiences, a place where the ancestors invested their lives and souls.

The plaque dedicated to Windradyne in Brucedale's far corner, near the ghost gum, is testament to that. Suttor's grandmother unveiled the plaque almost sixty-five years ago—a conscious act of remembering when Indigenous people weren't recognised as citizens, and some were, at death, still refused burial in consecrated ground. It reads:

THE RESTING PLACE OF WINDRADYNE,
ALIAS 'SATURDAY'
LAST CHIEF OF THE ABORIGINALS
FIRST A TERROR, BUT LATER A FRIEND
TO THE SETTLERS.
DIED OF WOUNDS RECEIVED IN A TRIBAL
ENCOUNTER, 1835
'A TRUE PATRIOT'
THIS PLAQUE WAS UNVEILED BY
MRS ROY SUTTOR
OF BRUCEDALE, 25TH APRIL, 1954

The date of death is incorrect. But that is irrelevant. It's the date of dedication I find so conspicuous. I can't help wondering if, dedicated thirty-six years after the Great War ended, in a district that had hundreds of Anzac veterans and fatalities, the plaque represents a somewhat more defiant act of commemoration. Regardless, it's symbolic of the tensions at the core of Australian national identity by which Anzac is afforded its claim at the expense of so very much else—not least 60 000 years of Indigenous civilisation and the frontier wars that raged at home.

Windradyne is rightly recognised in the area around Brucedale as a patriot for defending *country* from the British invader post 1788. Yet it's in 1788 and that invader's son—the Anzac, who made his name invading yet another country under British flag from the sea—that Australia invests so much of its patriotic sentiment.

With the end of the festival of Anzac 100, which rolled to a close on Remembrance

Day 2018, is it too much to hope that Australian commemoration hereafter takes a more solemn turn, away from the eulogising politicians and the sound-and-light shows? Is it too much to hope that other extraordinary elements of our continent and its history—the enduring civilisation and remarkable survival against the odds of Indigenous people; Australia's global precociousness on women's suffrage and workers' rights; the tension between our multiculturalism and treatment of refugees; a wilderness that's the envy of the world and the pioneering activism to protect it; and our country's early role as a global multilateralist—will no longer be shrouded in the darkness of the Anzac eclipse?

I hope.

Though for the moment, Anzac still seems to have its python grip on politics, if not always public imagination.

From Windradyne's grave, it's just a couple of hours as the eagle flies to the Tomb of the Unknown Australian Soldier at the war memorial. At the invitation of the memorial's director, Brendan Nelson, politicians are invited to spend time, supposedly alone, in the great stone-and-glass dome at the memorial's heart. There, on hands and knees, they wipe the dust from the unknown soldier's tomb—supposedly a private act of patriotism that is, nonetheless, sometimes captured on film.

One politician, Craig Kelly, explained:

To undertake such a task on a cold Canberra morning inside the Hall of Memory with the rising sun shining through the stained-glass panels was a very, very special and moving experience which I will always treasure. I would encourage all my parliamentary colleagues on both sides to take up this offer from Brendan Nelson and have the experience that I had.[24]

America has a long tradition of such patriotic expression. Congressmen like to be photographed cleaning, with soap and water, the names on the Vietnam Veterans Memorial in Washington.

There seems to me to be a strongly performative patriotic element to this, one that stirs unease in me. Notwithstanding the respect due to Australian personnel who die in training or on an operation, and the public element of what is purportedly an act of deeply personal and private reflection, precisely which other characters from our national story are afforded such treatment in death? Not our former prime ministers and governors-general. Nor is there an official monument to the frontier war dead in our national capital to be polished of dust; the war memorial stubbornly refuses to tell their story, and the nation tramples ever more recklessly, wilfully, on the sensibilities and mourning rites of Indigenous people every 26 January.

The unknown soldier has his due at the war memorial. But such national dignity and recognition is denied to the oldest known Australian: Mungo Man, a modern Indigenous human of this continent, at least

40 000 years old, whose bones geologist Jim Bowler found in the Willandra Lakes region of New South Wales in 1974. For forty-three years, to Bowler's chagrin, the remains of the man he discovered were kept in boxes at a university and later at the National Museum of Australia's storage facility in the outer Canberra suburb of Mitchell. Bowler, now in his late eighties, fought for decades to have the remains respectfully repatriated. In 2017 they were finally returned to the dry lakes, in a box made of precious red gum wood that Bowler and his wife Joan donated. But there is no grave for Mungo Man, no shiny stone memorial dedicated to him and from which to buff the dust. His coffin is kept in the basement of a visitor centre. This is hard to fathom given the remains are the oldest in

the world identifiably belonging to a modern man, a person who, tens of thousands of years ago, was given ceremonial funerary rites with fire and ochre.

Bowler is a former Catholic seminarian. I've spoken to him for hours about his discovery, about precisely what the sophisticated belief systems and civilisation inherent in Mungo Man—who lived some 36 000 years before the pyramids of Giza were built—bequeath to Australia. Bowler tells me: 'The anointing of the body in that nature is the sort of ritual that would be acceptable in any cathedral today. And there you've got the fire, think the smoke and the incense … so to have that in our backyard 40 000 years ago, there's nowhere else in the world that happens … think of it in the context of cultural continuity

of the present Aboriginal people. Not even …
the Indigenous people of Africa … have that
connection to anything like that continuity
of culture. So we [Australia] are sitting on an
extraordinarily privileged place in humanity.
The story of humanity is in the story of those
Mungo people. We are cosmophiles—we are
cosmopholic. We are connected to the cosmos. This is what you find in that situation,
that ritual. These were people of the sun and
the stars and the very landscape they lived in'.

If Mungo Man's story—his beliefs, his rit-
uals, his close connection to the beginning of
modern humanity—is central to understanding the cosmos, so, too, must be his *country*,
the Australian continent.

The story of the cosmos and Mungo Man
is quite mind-bending and challenging. But

Mungo Man's life is also a precious, uniquely Australian certainty that now freights my own appreciation and love of Australia with a meaning as deep as time itself.

How so? Indigenous belief in an animated earth and solar system, where totemic animals and other spirit beings made everything—and in so doing became part of the earth's story—are inextricably linked to the ancients of this continent and the world. Mungo Man's antiquity is central to that human beginning. He and his contemporaries are in the songlines that criss-cross the continent, understood and sung by contemporary Indigenous people *country*-wide. So, in Indigenous cosmology, Mungo Man is the closest modern human to Australia's—and the world's—beginning.

Bowler was never what he'd call an 'ideal seminarian'. Yet he retains a faith rooted in Celtic mysticism: 'I've rejected a lot of the dogmatic bullshit that we were taught at [Catholic] school. But early Celtic tradition was very different from the Roman Catholic Church. Early Celtic tradition is a monastic tradition I relate to. In those days the land was animated. There were elves and fairies and the dreaded Banshee'.

Bowler was implying an obvious parallel between early Christian and Indigenous mysticism. Yet his words still echo in me with a profound resonance as I walk about a continent so storied, one with a spirituality and civilisation history as deep as it is ancient. And as I do so, I think: *this is common ground—if only more non-Indigenous people would accept the invitation to stop, think about and proudly accept that this is all part of a narrative bringing their lives and those of their ancestors into perspective too.*

This is Australia's truest story. It comes from the heart of our continent, not some other shore. If Australia would project this remarkable aspect of its being with half the energy it dedicates to Anzac and European arrival, how very different, how nuanced and rich, the complexion of our patriotism would be.

It is heartbreaking that Australia under the former Turnbull government blithely rejected a generous invitation to claim as national bedrock the continent's sixty millennia of Indigenous sovereignty and civilisation.

The *Uluru Statement from the Heart* was not, as some white politicians would have us fear, a scattergun claim of Indigenous rights and demands. No—it was a decorous petition, a wise articulation of Indigenous sentiment drawn from broad community consultations in response to a government question: what constitutional recognition do you want? The statement was an elegant expression of diplomacy from Indigenous people who've never been afforded the same.

'We invite you to walk with us in a movement of the Australian people for a better future', the statement reads.[25]

Here was a once-in-a-generation *makarrata*—an Indigenous invitation to unify after struggle by agreeing to a process of historical truth telling and a voice to federal parliament whose shape (while never intended to be a third chamber, as Turnbull and his ministers untruthfully asserted) was not predetermined. It was an overture to the nation to forge a new Australian identity that reflects Indigenous experiences of pre- and post-colonial history, land management, culture, science and cosmology.

It was composed with an acute mind for an imminent Australian republic—one that must not abandon blackfellas … yet again.

'With substantive constitutional change and structural reform, we believe this ancient sovereignty can shine through as a fuller expression of Australia's nationhood', the *Uluru Statement* reads.[26]

Turnbull, once bitten while driving the Australian republican movement off a proverbial cliff at the 1999 referendum, due, in part, to some of the temperamental and managerial flaws that characterised his prime ministership, these days declares himself an 'Elizabethan' and big constitutional reform too damned difficult.

Federal Labor, rhetorically at least, is more engaged with the aspirations of both Uluru and the republican movement—and with the notion, perhaps, that it's time to look elsewhere in addition to Britannia and Howard's sheriff, the United States, as Australia rethinks its sense of 21st-century self. But big questions linger about Labor's capacity to turn further away than their opponents from the dual—and often interchangeable—nation-defining narratives of British settlement and Anzac. In Australian major party politics today, while there are occasional outbreaks of dissent on questions of national identity, publicly rethinking either the big exclusive national celebration of non-Indigenous Australia on 26 January, Invasion Day, or the veracity of attaching national birth to 25 April, is pretty much heresy.

So, what will be the politicians' narrative about our inevitable republic? Will it merely be a box ticked—a largely symbolic change that cuts the cord with the Windsors before resuming normal transmission? Or will our constitutional independence be seized as the golden opportunity it could be to promote a broader, more inclusive national pride transcendent of the bipartisan shibboleths we've clung to for so long?

Most importantly, will the movement towards an Australian republic make central to its quest the invitation from Uluru to 'make ancient sovereignty a fuller expression of Australian nationhood'?

As a republican, I'd sometimes wondered why many of my Indigenous acquaintances were ambivalent and complacent about, even hostile towards, a republic. It wasn't until I started delving into frontier history—for all its contemporary social, physical, economic and psychological reverberations through First Nations—that I began to appreciate why. Many asked, would an Australian republic disavow the violence committed against us? Would there be a genuine reckoning with our troubling history under an Australian head of state? How would Indigenous outcomes be improved?

It was the same thing I'd repeatedly heard when the politicians started kicking around the notion of some symbolic constitutional recognition of Indigenous peoples—taking the lead of John Howard, never a true friend of blackfellas, as he was poised to lose his seat, ironically named after Aboriginal leader Bennelong, in 2007.

As 'recognition' became part of the political orthodoxy—with its endless committees, the top-down Recognise movement costing tens upon tens of millions of dollars, and the blithe acceptance by many journalists ordinarily unconcerned with Indigenous affairs that, well, it must be an okay thing given

it's all so bipartisan with the white pollies—
I heard more and more black voices asking:
why would I want to be recognised in the settler state's founding document?

Fair point.

As Waanyi and Jaru medical anthropologist Gregory Phillips pointed out in 2018, 'I
believe a republic will be good for Australia,
but not if it is simply an act of recolonising
Aboriginal and Torres Strait Islander peoples
under normalised white supremacy ...'.[27]
As for constitutional recognition, Phillips
writes that it 'is about Aboriginal and Torres
Strait Islander peoples being included on
white people's terms into a white constitution and power structure—it is the crumbs
off the white man's table, while they stay in
power'.[28]

The *Uluru Statement*, it should be remembered, rejected any symbolic recognition in favour of constitutionally enshrining 'the voice'—a concept the government seems to lack either the imaginative capacity or the will to even conceptualise. The government, having asked the question, found distasteful the answer, and so it cynically misrepresented the statement's response. Turnbull's ministers disrespectfully rubbished the Uluru consensus while the then PM feigned reserved judgement, months later dismissing the Uluru answer via press release. As prime minister, Scott Morrison, his notions of reconciliation reflected in a planned $50 million aquatic monument to Captain Cook on the shore of Botany Bay in his electorate, may be no improvement.

Might the eventual republic make central to a new Australia its Indigenous sovereignty, and prioritise better outcomes for Aboriginal and Torres Strait Islander peoples? Will it embrace the offer from Uluru to walk hand in hand with black Australia to redefine Australian nationhood? Will republicanism hold the black voice to parliament as a central tenet of the new Australia it seeks?

The republican movement's leaders have said often enough that they respect the Indigenous consensus out of Uluru, just as they insist that they want Aboriginal identity and rights to be a central part of an Australian republic—but they don't want to 'colonise' or overshadow the recognition movement.

Megan Davis, a Cobble Cobble woman and constitutional law academic, was a member of the referendum council that gauged Indigenous sentiment on recognition and helped formulate the *Uluru Statement*, before reading it publicly. In 2018, Davis wrote:

> The least glamorous part of Australian republicanism has always been the question of Aboriginal sovereignty. And it is yet to be reconciled … We run the very real risk of a republic that renders the First Peoples invisible in the same way the constitutional monarchy did. And when we object they will blithely say, 'That was under the old system, this is the new Australia'. And for many mob … the morning after a successful referendum nothing will change.[29]

The concerns about some exclusive 'white' Australian republic that leaves Aboriginal and

Torres Strait Islander peoples behind are not solely or even predominantly an Indigenous preoccupation. Progressive Australians, regardless of political affiliation, have in the past decade become more engaged with Indigenous culture, the tragedies of near extinction through frontier violence and stolen generations, and with spiritual beliefs and activism, than might've been imaginable for Donald Horne in 1964. Or, indeed, for William Stanner, when, four years later, the revered anthropologist came up with the still resonant 'great Australian silence' to describe this country's Aboriginal history void.[30]

As a republican, I'm not persuaded by a campaign that merely runs in parallel to Indigenous interests; I want one that will help guarantee the voice to parliament, a formal process of historical truth telling, and, not least, help deliver better social, economic and lifestyle outcomes for Aboriginal and Torres Strait Islander peoples.

If that's a tougher republic to attain, so be it.

Mark McKenna, one of Australia's pre-eminent contemporary historians, has articulated the need for some concentrated introversion when it comes to forging a republican national identity:

> Yet for all the time republicans have imagined that the question of the country's independence was anchored solely in its relationship with Britain and her monarchy. We have looked outwards rather than within, knowing what we want to reject but being less certain about what we want to create in the monarchy's absence.[31]

The 'business as usual' minimalist model of 1980s and 1990s Turnbull republicanism won't do, McKenna says:

> We have already 'broken away' and become an independent nation except in two crucial respects: we are without an Australian head of state and we have yet to anchor our vision of popular sovereignty in the continent's Indigenous antiquity as the Uluru Statement from the Heart invites us to do. This is the true source of a more mature and independent Australia—the grounding of our sovereignty on our own soil, in the songlines and histories of an ancient island continent.[32]

It's a crisp, still Friday night in Sydney, one of those evenings when the harbour and everything around it seem to parade with an outrageous, seductive beauty—natural, sculptural, neon and glowing. It's not where I was born or even where I've spent most of my life. But since moving to this place of sparkling magnificence, of blue sky, temperate air and water—water everywhere!—I've been captivated. For so many visitors, the allure comes from the monuments to modernity, especially the bridge, one of the world's most distinctive, and Jørn Utzon's sails of white tile upon the point where the first governor, Arthur Phillip, 'invited' Bennelong to live in a purpose-built hut—the Englishman's 'guest', as some Australian history teachers and books instructed me without irony.

But long before the bridge, long before Utzon, this was already a place of coveted, sometimes contested, beauty for the local custodians. The first locals even had their own monuments: middens of shell—oyster, mussel, scallop, pipi—some up to 12 metres high, that testified to dozens of millennia of ancestral lives. One of those monuments stood about where the Opera House is. However, the early fleets arrived without lime for concrete. And as the Port Jackson settlement voraciously expanded, so, too, the shell monuments were correspondingly hacked to pieces for building lime. It's an irresistible metaphor: the diminution of Indigenous Australian civilisation as Europe concretes over it.

I'm thinking about all of this, as I always do when I'm by Circular Quay, on this Friday night as we take our seats in the Opera House for a performance of the Central Australian

Aboriginal Women's Choir, The Song
Keepers. The choir comprises thirty-two
women and two men from six Western Desert
communities who sing in their Australian languages some of Christianity's oldest poetry.
The German Lutheran missionaries of the
nineteenth century brought God and sacred
Christian song to Hermannsburg. They
translated the hymns into Pitjantjatjara and
Arrarnte and taught the locals to sing them.

The performance is a celebration of trans-
cultural wonder, of different Australias,
earthed in the same ancient continent, com-
ing together. It has a mostly non-Indigenous
audience howling with joy, clapping hands
and stamping feet.

The conductor, the enigmatic Guyana-
born Morris Stuart, implores the audience to

consider the endurance of the languages we are hearing, holding, as they do, the history and integrity of the oldest human civilisation. During an earlier performance in another city, he'd explained, 'We should be whoop-eeing and hollering and throwing cartwheels that we're in the place where our ancestors have preserved this for us'.

Our ancestors.

The choir is sonorous and soul-shifting, its hymns serene. It is 'Kumbayah, my Lord', sung in Arrarnte, that brings the greatest gasps of appreciation. Next comes 'Waltzing Matilda'. For all its oddity and, in so many other deliveries, cheesiness, this song is hard to rival for colonial Australianness. White Australia regards it as an old, old song—a de facto national anthem. But it's actually new again when rendered in ancient Pitjantjatjara replete with the 'baaaa' of the jumbuck in the tuckerbag.

And it's as if the Concert Hall of the Opera House has just passed through its very own giant 'hole in the wall' of realisation, just like I did out in the Arafura that time with the Yolngu. The hall is overwhelmed. Many around us are sobbing at the dawning—or reaffirmation—of consciousness that this land, all of this *country* around us, hosts an ancient human and spiritual mystery that can incorporate all of our faiths, beliefs and histories, individual and shared.

And at this moment it has never been clearer to me that my expression of love for this remarkable country—my Australian patriotism—will always draw its deepest meaning from *country* itself.

Notes

1   Horne, Donald, *The Lucky Country*, 2nd revised ed.,
    Angus & Robertson, 1965, p. 4.
2   Horne, p. 27.
3   Horne, p. 145.
4   Horne, p. 5.
5   Film Australia, 'Donald Horne', *Australian Biography*
    series, 1992, http://www.australianbiography.gov.
    au/subjects/horne/intertext4.html
6   Stephens, David, 'Why is Australia spending so much
    more on the Great War centenary than any other
    country?', John Menadue – Pearls and Irritations,
    20 June 2015, https://johnmenadue.com/david-
    stephens-why-is-australia-spending-so-much-more-
    on-the-great-war-centenary-than-any-other-country
7   Cochrane, Peter, 'The past is not sacred: the "history
    wars" over Anzac', *The Conversation*, 25 April 2015,
    http://theconversation.com/the-past-is-not-sacred-
    the-history-wars-over-anzac-38596
8   Ibid.
9   Quoted in Daley, Paul, 'Lest we forget the horror',
    The Sydney Morning Herald, 24 April 2011, https://

www.smh.com.au/politics/federal/lest-we-forget-the-horror-20110423-1ds7f.html

10   *The Australian*, 'The Anzac sentiment defies central planning', 26 April 2013, https://www.theaustralian.com.au/opinion/editorials/the-anzac-sentiment-defies-central-planning/news-story/8cf6589526baddbd854e68c894516449?sv=d125f0dee10148458cd76538e46b0241

11   Hunter, Fergus, '"It's not going to happen": Barnaby Joyce rejects push for Aboriginal body in constitution', *The Sydney Morning Herald*, 29 May 2017, https://www.smh.com.au/politics/federal/its-not-going-to-happen-barnaby-joyce-rejects-push-for-aboriginal-body-in-constitution-20170529-gwf5ld.html

12   Keating, Paul, 'Redfern Speech (Year for the World's Indigenous People)', Redfern Park, Sydney, 10 December 1992, https://aso.gov.au/media/docs/Redfern_Speech10121992.pdf

13   Department of the Prime Minister and Cabinet, 'Transcript of the Prime Minister the Hon John Howard MP opening address to the Australian Reconciliation Convention – Melbourne', PM Transcripts, 26 May 1997, https://pmtranscripts.pmc.gov.au/release/transcript-10361

14   McPhedran, Ian, *The Amazing SAS*, Harper Collins, 2005, p. 139.

15   Department of the Prime Minister and Cabinet, 'Address at Anzac Day Dawn Service Gallipoli', PM Transcripts, 25 April 2005, https://pmtranscripts. pmc.gov.au/release/transcript-21719

16   Daley, Paul, 'Cronulla riots: there's still the capacity for Anzac name to be taken in vain', *The Guardian*, 11 December 2013, https://www.the-guardian.com/world/postcolonial/2013/dec/11/still-capacity-for-cronulla-riot

17   Quoted in ibid.

18   Quoted in ibid.

19   Johnston, George, *My Brother Jack*, Imprint Classics, Angus & Robertson, 1988, p. 2.

20   Pascoe, Bruce, 'Aboriginal people do what we must to survive; 1967 didn't change that', ABC Online, 25 May 2017, http://www.abc.net.au/news/2017-05-25/bruce-pascoe-doesnt-think-much-about-the-1967-referendum/8349860

21   Gullett, Henry, *The Official History of Australia in the War of 1914–1918: Sinai and Palestine* (vol. VII), Angus & Robertson, 1937, p. 103.

22   Hill, Ernestine, 'Man whose gun keeps white men safe in wilds', *Sunday Sun and Guardian*, 5 February 1933.

23   Suttor, William Henry, *Australian Stories Retold and Sketches of Country Life*, Glyndwr Whalan, 1887.

24   Kelly, Craig, 'Constituency statement: Australian
      War Memorial, National Boer War Memorial', House
      Debates, OpenAustralia, 22 May 2017, https://www.
      openaustralia.org.au/debates/?id=2017-05-22.142.1

25   *Uluru Statement from the Heart*, 26 May 2017, https://
      www.documentcloud.org/documents/3755370-
      ULURU-STATEMENT-FROM-the-HEART.html

26   Ibid.

27   Phillips, Gregory, 'No republic without a soul: exor-
      cising the ghosts of colonialism', *Griffith Review 60
      – First Things First*, edited by Julianne Schultz and
      Sandra Phillips, Griffith University, p. 97.

28   Ibid., p. 103.

29   Davis, Megan, 'The republic is an Aboriginal
      issue', *The Monthly*, April 2018, https://www.
      themonthly.com.au/issue/2018/april/1522
      501200/megan-davis/republic-aboriginal-issue

30   Stanner, William, *After the Dreaming: Black and
      White Australians—an Anthropologist's View*, Boyer
      Lectures series, ABC, 1969.

31   McKenna, Mark, *Quarterly Essay: Moment of
      Truth—History and Australia's Future*, no. 69, Black
      Inc., 2018, p. 66.

32   Ibid.